Create CLARITY:

Self-Coach The Yorkshire Way

by

Ruth Rathband

'Clarity is Power.'

Billy Cox

'It's a lack of clarity that causes chaos and frustration.'

Steve Maraboli

'Clarity affords focus.'

Thomas Leonard

'Clarity of purpose trumps knowledge.'

Clayton Christensen

Contents

Background

Born in **Doncaster, South Yorkshire**, in the year Harold Macmillan said, 'we've never had it so good,' that was certainly my take on life, as a kid, growing up in the 60s.

Always a coal fire ablaze in the hearth, smoking chimneys, great home cooking, and nothing more to worry about than itchy balaclavas and Tuf shoes that were impossible to wear out. And joy of joys, stories everywhere: in the books borrowed from the local library, old action movies on the rented TV, and the occasional treasured visit to the cinema.

Fast forward to the 1980s, and another memory pops up of a young mum running around like a headless chicken trying to write a self-help book for other women! My first thought was - *'What was I on?'*

With a busy family life, and job to boot, where did I find the time, or the inclination, to write a shopping list, let alone a self-help book. And what, at that tender age, did I think I knew? I can only surmise that an embarrassingly heady dose of **Yorkshire 'know-it-all,'** and the exuberance of youth, played a part. As well as, perhaps, intuitively knowing that I would write such a book one day.

This memory, by connecting me back to my younger, unfiltered self, showed me that the traits and desires that drove me then, still drive me now. For as long as I can remember, I have always had a passion for reading, writing, and learning. I wanted to become a social worker (and save the world), and then a teacher (and educate the world), and then a counsellor (and heal the world) - but life and circumstance took me in another direction.

But, that ever-present thirst for knowledge led to degrees, diplomas, and countless courses on this and that.

'If you can't figure out your purpose, figure out your passion. For your passion will lead you right into your purpose.' **T. D. Jakes**

We've all been shaped (physically and emotionally) by nature and nurture and the ups and downs of a life lived. And through it all at your core remains the essence of what makes you that unique human being.

Whatever your life journey has been, the chances are, like me, you've been knocked off your perch from time to time.

Maybe there were times when, if you're honest, you may have seen it coming, and there were other times where, just like Del Boy falling through the bar, you were down and out before you knew it.

But, whatever your circumstance, whatever your age, wherever you are, whatever your gender or none, the power is within you, and always has been, to orchestrate change in your life.

Now, I know that you may be thinking, *'Well, if it was that simple, love, I'd have done it by now.'* With the possible addition of an expletive or two - especially if you're getting seriously fed up having travelled down a number of self-help routes which have failed to deliver any meaningful change for you.

So, let's be clear - reading a self-help book, no matter how amazing, informative, fun, or popular it may be, will not change your life one jot!

You may have a lovely time, smiling and nodding to

yourself, as you recognise and relate to so much of what is being presented.

You may feel uplifted because you are hearing stuff that you innately already know - with a few new gems thrown in along the way - if you're lucky.

This can be nourishing, as you recognise that the author, be they a celebrity, philosopher, psychologist, coach, counsellor, physician, scientist etc., speaks your language.

And they speak your language because they are knowledgeable (hopefully) about the human condition and how we tick. But that inner glow, and sense of understanding yourself better, will not change your life when you get to 'The End,' unless you put the book down, **get up and take action**.

'You are what you do, not what you say you'll do.' Carl Jung

Acquiring knowledge is just that: you acquire knowledge.

It is what you decide to do with that knowledge, that will determine whether your future will be any different to your past.

If you merely, pick up another self-help book and read that, then another, and another, well, you may become extremely knowledgeable, and probably be able to talk the talk, regarding self-coaching tools, ideas and techniques – but, yes, you knew this was coming – you need to walk the walk, if you are truly seeking transformation.

<u>So, why write (yet another) Self-Coaching book?</u>

Well, the answer is quite simple: I felt compelled to do so. A feeling from within; an intuitive nudge; an insatiable itch; however I looked at it - there would be no peace for me until the deed was done.

The background to all of this is, that after taking early retirement to finally 'live the dream,' and be a writer, I began to suspect that I had some **self-sabotaging behaviours (thoughts/feelings/actions)** that I could neither locate nor understand.

Having always seen myself as a decisive, self-assured person, I was not at all happy (that's putting it mildly) about finding myself 'stuck.'

In my search for answers, I began to learn about Life Coaching and the undisputed power of questions???

'You CAN teach an old dog new tricks!'

Ruth Rathband

www.ruthrathband.com

And my frustration began to be replaced by new and exciting ways of thinking, doing, and being: which just goes to prove that **you can teach 'an old dog new tricks!'**

Everything I began to learn about coaching made perfect sense to me. I experienced constant feelings of déjà vu – and this is not uncommon - though I appreciate that it might sound a tad dramatic.

But the reason for this is quite simple: coaching connects you back to yourself - a person that you already know pretty well. It helps you to unpick all the dross that builds up in life by giving you the skills to navigate your way to a place of understanding and **knowing**.

I wasn't expecting to find the clarity that I was seeking by simply 'going home.' But I did. Not home to Yorkshire: but to myself.

So, that insatiable itch began right there and then, when I began to study for a Diploma in Life Coaching and NLP (Neuro Linguistic Programming). As soon as I began to understand and know myself better, I also knew that it was possible for others to do the same. And I wanted to tell **'everyman and his dog'** that they could self-coach.

And so, the idea to create a straight-talking, light-hearted and inspiring guide to get people started on that journey, led to the toolkit: ***Create Clarity: Self-Coach the Yorkshire Way.***

Now, I grant you that to those in the personal development, personal transformation business, this may not sound like a great eureka moment. After all there are a vast number self-coaching books already out there, but what I wanted to develop was something that would appeal to those who had never heard of self-coaching, or who had little or no idea of what it was, or those who thought that this kind of thing was not for them – in other words 'not my cup of tea.'

I see **Create Clarity: Self-Coach The Yorkshire Way** as your starter for ten.

Where you end up, as in how free, fulfilled, successful, whole, creative, happy etc., you become is down to you.

My wish is that this toolkit will act as a **sign-post** that starts you on the road back to yourself; to being at ease within your own skin, and to open your mind to the belief that you can create the life you most desire.

This is a journey of self-discovery, self-awareness, self-motivation, self-belief, and self-care.

You, become your own self-coaching guru or detective.

So, whether you fancy being **a Sherlock, a Vera or a Van der Valk** (you decide), you are perfectly capable of taking what you learn here and making it just the beginning of your self-coaching journey.

Out there (I've listed some at the back of the book) is a vast array of great teachers who can't wait to share what they know, and accompany you on your way.

I would always recommend working your way through all the **FREE** stuff they offer first. Because as you begin to understand yourself better you will intuitively find yourself gravitating towards what speaks to you, and recognising what does not.

There may come a time when you want to sign-up for a course, or work one-to-one with a counsellor, a coach, an energy healer...

The point is that once you can pinpoint more accurately the sort of specialist help you do need (if any) you won't go wasting **valuable time and money** trying all manner of things that aren't right for you.

Being miserable and staying stuck in the [1]**'horrors of the half-known life'** can be addictive, and is an option, but so too is that feeling that you're on your way to becoming the version of you that you always knew you could be.

---

[1] Melville, Hermann, *Moby Dick*, 1851, Richard Bentley, London

The CLARITY Toolkit

C = Creating Spaces

Clear the decks: create spaces to evolve

L = Listening & Learning

Become a listener and a learner - not a judger

A = Acceptance, Awareness & Attraction

Understand your values and beliefs

R = Reality v Fake News

Challenge self-sabotaging thoughts

I = Integrity First

Live authentically: be honest and trustworthy

T = Tackling Tolerations

Develop extreme self-care: physical and mental

Y = Yesterday is Gone

Live in the 'perfect' present

How to use this Toolkit

I don't know what the trigger was that brought you to this toolkit but whatever it was I'm glad you're here.

And I'm glad you're here for two reasons:

- **You've acted** - you've made a decision to be here - so you've already taken the first step in coaching yourself;

- **I'm grateful** that you've trusted me to help you kick-start your self-coaching journey.

This toolkit is crammed with ideas, tools, and techniques for you to explore; however, do bear in mind that it will depend on **where** you are in your life, as to **what** will speak to you **when**. The power of self-coaching is not just present in lightbulb moments, but in the cumulative effect of developing the quality of your thinking (and as a consequence your actions) beyond where you are at present.

You can help yourself to get the most out of this toolkit by having:

- an **OPEN** mind

- a commitment to **ACT**

- a desire to connect/reconnect with your **INTUITIVE** self

- a willingness to **KNOW** yourself better

- a **SMILE** on your face…

So, let's start flexing that self-coaching muscle (no matter how flabby it is).

You decide which module to start with.

You can work your way through the modules – 'Creating Spaces' to 'Yesterday is Gone' – or you can scan down the list and start with the one that jumps out at you.

Trust your instinct.

And then move onto the next one that jumps out at you - and so on.

As you work your way through these modules, you will see that they are linked – not like links in a chain, but more like facets on a crystal; so that when you focus on one you can see a connection to another, and then another.

So, give it your best shot.

I believe in you.

I hope you do too!

C = Create Spaces

'Be steady and well-ordered in your life so that you can be fierce and original in your work.' **Gustave Flaubert**

Clear the decks – create spaces in which to evolve.

We all occupy spaces. We live, work, drive, eat, and sleep in spaces: whether it's a car, an office, a house, a bedroom etc.

But what we may not always appreciate is how much the *physical* spaces that we inhabit affect us.

Why create spaces?

Because things grow in spaces, **not** in weed infested ground, cluttered homes, cars, works stations, or minds bursting with over-thinking and over-critical thoughts.

And, even if you feel that you're pretty well organised on the decluttering and organising front, then consider taking it to a higher plane. The knock-on effect is truly spectacular.

You will be amazed at how you feel.

But this is not a one-off process with a beginning, a middle, and an end. This is ongoing.

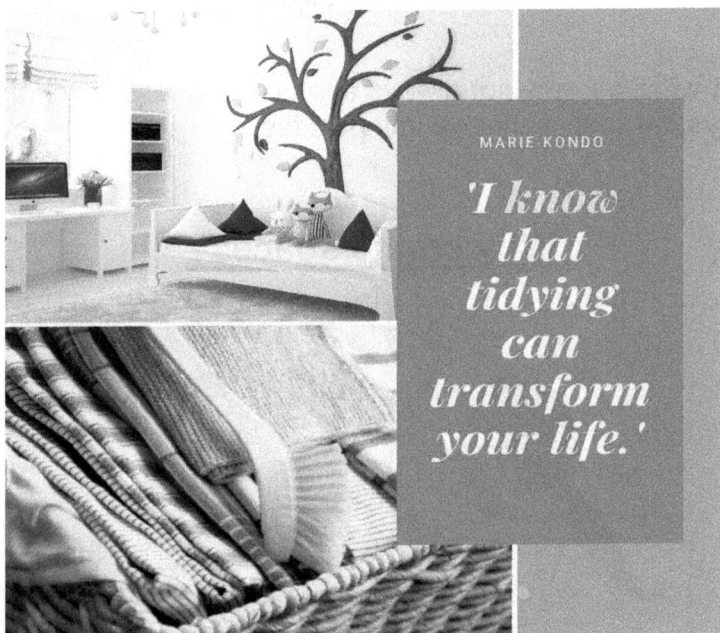

MARIE KONDO

'I know that tidying can transform your life.'

Once you've gone through all the spaces that impact on your life.

Guess what?

In order to maintain that feeling of air flowing through your home, your car, your thoughts, and ideas… you'll need to keep topping it up because you won't want to lose it.

How to get started

Clean up! Tidy up! Get rid!

That's it in a nutshell.

Know your possessions, and know where they are.

So, when you're looking for those amazing scissors with the yellow handle you know exactly where they are. No time wasting. Brilliant.

The time it takes to get this decluttering and organising done will come back to you tenfold.

You will know, hand on heart, if you've got a big job on your hands or not?

Either way nothing will change if you don't start.

So just start.

Even if it's baby steps – just keep taking them.

Remember, you're in charge.

They are YOUR spaces.

This is YOUR stuff.

You CAN do it.

From the off you will feel the weight lifting; as though the physical weight of the stuff being removed or rearranged makes you feel lighter.

You'll begin to find space, time, and moments

during your day for yourself.

Just imagine - sitting in your clutter free home and breathing in new thoughts and ideas.

Get some professional help - if you need it.

If you seriously struggle to part with chipped crockery and bent knives, then maybe you'll need to be parted from some serious money to get you going.

Not the best incentive in the world - but if you're paying a professional organiser then you'd better shape up.

FAST!

On the other hand, if someone close to you is willing – family member, close friend - to offer moral support, and hopefully challenge your need for keeping that wonky fork - then this could help.

However, do bear in mind, if you find that you are attached to stuff, masses of stuff (that looks like rubbish to everyone else), then I would encourage you to explore why?

Take the time to ask yourself the question. Why do I need to keep this?

If it is for some sentimental reason then ok – **up to a limit**.

But if you are struggling to part with *anything* then you might need to explore this in more depth.

'When you come across something that you cannot throw away, think carefully about its true purpose in your life... by letting (it) go with gratitude, you will be able to truly put the things you own, and your life, in order.' **Marie Kondo**

Calling all you **hoarders** with stuff in lock-ups, lofts, garages and storage facilities - go and check out what

you've got!

Have you been paying to keep stuff you haven't seen, or possibly can't even remember what you've got, for months - even years?

If so, the chances are you don't need it.

What do you intend to do with this stuff? If you don't need it now, why will you need it in the future?

If there's a good answer – great. If not then save yourself some money and get rid. *'It might come in handy,'* is not a great answer.

Like any skill you want to get good at, practise is the key.

You will find, very quickly, that your decision making will improve.

You will get better at knowing what you truly

need/want in your life, and it probably won't stop at just your physical possessions!

And *please* don't leave stuff for your kids to sort out when you're dead and gone.

Do them a huge favour while you're still around and go through all that you own.

Pass on the treasures.

Treasure the memories.

And don't freak them out with bizarre conditions like, *'you've got to keep your grandad's teeth in pride of place on the mantelpiece!'*

FREE yourself and your loved ones from unnecessary clutter.

Learn to let go.

Don't allow the size of the task to intimidate you.

Just start.

Have a vision for each room. Make a few notes. Don't take a week drawing a beautiful image. Hold the image in your head.

Clear and recycle newspapers. Sort the books.

Find a space for storing umbrellas, wellies…

By starting the motivation will follow.

The only thing that's not an option is doing nothing; unless of course, you're not really looking to change anything?

Be honest.

If you're just giving this process lip service then you'll never know how amazing creating spaces will make you feel.

You could begin with just 30 mins twice a week – if you stick with this – you'll see change and the chances are you'll want to do more, more often.

The momentum of the energy that you will experience by creating new life-changing, life-enhancing habits will propel you forward. So, no more procrastination, discussion, scheduling for tomorrow or next Monday.

Put the kettle on, and in the time it takes to make a brew, throw out a few things from that overflowing kitchen drawer that's full of junk.

Yes, that one!

L = Listening & Learning

'If you're not listening, you're not learning.'
Lyndon B Johnson

Why listen and learn?

Because when we listen, truly listen, without judgement or preconceived ideas we learn more than we ever imagined.

We develop and strengthen our ability to empathise with others and the diverse world in which we live.

As our information gathering and decision-making skills are enhanced, our life choices will stand on sure foundations and lead to positive outcomes.

How to get started

Most of us like to think we are good listeners; but in general, quite the opposite is true.

So, if you've never explored the idea that you might *not* be a good listener, then the chances are you're *not* a good listener!

Think about what *you* are thinking about, when you are supposedly 'listening' to someone else?

Here are a few things to mull over.

Have you already made up your mind about what **you think** about the speaker and the topic?

Are you really listening to what they have to say, or are you simply sifting for evidence to justify the view that you already have?

This isn't listening.

Are you thinking about your response, a funny quip, a piece of advice, a question, before they've finished speaking?

This isn't listening.

Is your mind wandering? Have you switched off from what they are saying? Thinking about what you fancy for dinner?

This isn't listening.

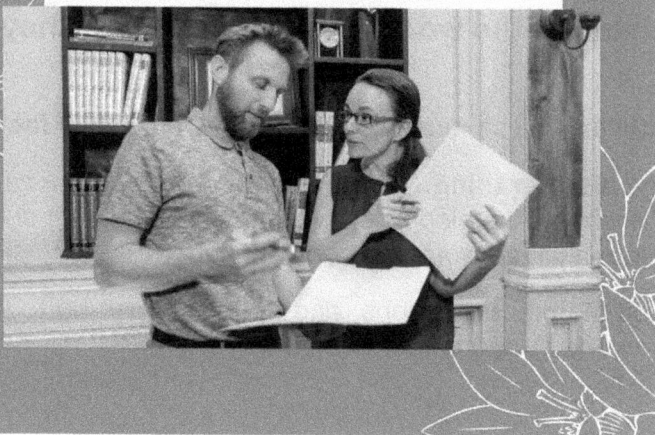
'I'm sorry I wasn't listening. Could you repeat everything you've ever said to me since you started working here?'

Are you constantly checking or texting on your phone?

This certainly isn't listening!

If you listen with an open, non-judgemental mind from the off, you could be amazed at what you hear, and what you think about what they are saying. You may, however, keep your original thoughts on the matter, but at least if you've actively listened to another point of view, you will understand more about the other person, and why they think the way they do.

So put your listening ears on!

There's also a real possibility that you might discover something new about those closest to you.

It is so easy to think you know someone well.

Try listening with your full attention when they next speak to you.

Listen to the words they use and how they say them.

It will tell you so much about how they are **really feeling**.

And another thing... We close many doors to our capacity to learn and develop when we stand in judgement of others before a single word has been spoken.

Drop the preconceptions, and the bias, open up to seeing the world through other people's eyes.

You might be surprised by what you see...

A bit about LEARNING

Learning new stuff is good for you.

'You'll never be bored when you try something new. There's really no limit to what you can do.' **Dr Seuss**

Actually, the subject matter is in some ways immaterial.

Obviously, if you want specific skills to go after a new job, change careers etc - then what you might be interested in learning is probably pretty clear.

However, if you're not up for any kind of formal learning, then why not think about things that you are interested in, and follow your nose to gain more information about these subjects.

Start exploring...

Learning is an incredible tool that not only nourishes and feeds us mentally and spiritually, but also builds **self-confidence, self-reliance and self-belief.**

Make learning a new habit.

Encourage yourself to learn (something/anything) and work on becoming more **curious** about all manner of things.

Get interested in things going on around you and you will become a more interesting person.

QUESTIONS are the key here.

When you start asking **questions** of yourself you begin a journey of self-discovery; when you start asking **questions** of others (and **LISTEN** to what they have to say) you begin opening your mind to new ways of thinking, doing, and being.

And we grow intellectually when we broaden our minds through learning; allowing us to be more open, insightful, and receptive to the opportunities that life presents.

How far you go with this is entirely up to you.

But be in no doubt that you will feel empowered when you improve your listening skills, stay curious and **make learning your new best friend.**

A bit about JUDGING

It's basically a bad idea to get on your high-horse and stand in judgement of others – we kind of already know this - but it doesn't seem to stop us.

There's an element to judging situations and people - which comes from our intuitive self-preservation part.

This is natural. It's designed to keep us safe.

You feel uneasy in someone's company, you enter a room and the atmosphere feels wrong: it's negative, a bad vibe, and your internal alarm bell starts ringing.

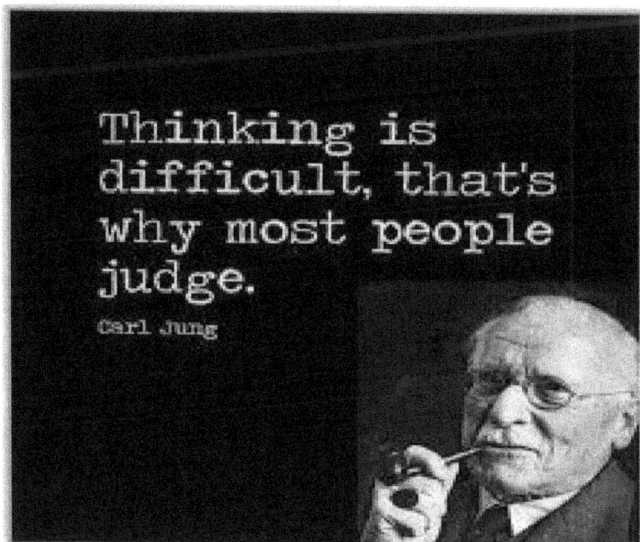

Thinking is difficult, that's why most people judge.

Carl Jung

So, let's be clear here, I'm not suggesting that you override this invaluable sense to detect an environment, or people, who are basically not good for you.

What I'm talking about, is judging based on bias, fear, preconceived prejudices, and believed falsities; because when you build, and live, behind these types of barriers you deny yourself much of the joy and wonder of life.

If you accept the premise that we are all capable of judging, then you can start to recognise when you have put your 'judger head on' (Worzel Gummidge style).

There's no need to beat yourself up about this: just accept it.

THEN get curious, and start asking yourself some great questions.

- **Why do I think this?**

- **Where did this thinking come from?**

- **What are the facts?**

- **Where is the proof?**

- **Am I making assumptions?**

By asking yourself these types of questions you are becoming **more aware and more conscious** about why you think what you think.

Instead of staying fixed in your thinking, teach yourself to be more thoughtful about your own thoughts.

But, remember, this isn't a game show so you don't have to come up with an answer straightaway.

You might need to give yourself some time to step back, press pause, and look at the issue more objectively.

Imagine that you have just put new 'objective' specs on – and you can now see more clearly.

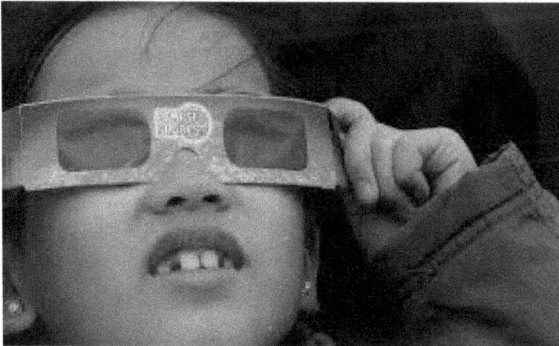

Observe yourself.

Question yourself.

The answers will come, because they are within you…

A = Acceptance, Awareness & Attraction

'To do good things in the world, first you must know who you are and what gives meaning to your life.' Robert Browning

Why accept?

'Time doesn't heal everything but acceptance will heal everything.'

Unknown

Because accepting where you are lifts a great burden from your shoulders and allows for clearer thinking.

Acceptance is often the place from which you can start to build a new and better way forward; for in accepting, you put yourself in a position to explore options previously denied to you by the rigidity of unacceptance.

Acceptance is not passive.

Acceptance is not giving in.

In many ways it can be seen as quite the opposite; especially when you're saying 'ok' to a situation that you don't like.

Because with acceptance comes freedom.

'LOVE what you HAVE, before life teaches you to LOVE what you LOST.'
Leonardo DiCaprio

#gratitude

This freedom allows you to summon *all* your resources (from within and outside yourself) to create and develop a new way forward.

You are now in a position of strength to bring about change.

How to get started

Gratitude can be a good place to start.

When you're focussing on things that just aren't right in your life, it can be a game changer to come at it from a completely different direction.

So, how about reminding yourself of what's good in your life.

As the old saying goes '*don't forget to count your blessings.*'

Take a minute first thing in the morning and last thing at night to remind yourself of some of the good things already present in your life e.g. your pasta making skills, your amazing teeth, your kids, your best friend, your full beard, your smelly dog, your fab granny, your long legs, your crazy cat...

Bringing *everything and anything* that adds value to your life to the forefront of your mind, on a regular basis, helps to ensure that you don't take these 'blessings' for granted.

Giving gratitude some serious welly will lift your mood, make you smile, and help you to focus from a more 'glass half-full' perspective.

Acceptance also develops **awareness.**

And when you raise your **awareness** new and exciting ways of achieving your goals will reveal themselves.

Perhaps ways that you didn't even know existed.

A bit about AWARENESS

In order to become more **aware** and **self-aware** – have a crack at getting to know **YOU** better.

Obviously, you already know a ton of stuff about yourself.

But how often do you actually give much thought to the question: Who am I?

Well, your starter for 10 could be: where you were born, when you were born, where you went to school, how tall you are, how many siblings you have, what job you do/did, where you go on holiday, what's your name, what's your address, what colour are your eyes…

Answers to these types of questions only represent you as a black and white sketch.

The real answer to 'who am I?' is what is revealed when you start to colour in this sketch with all the intangible bits about you: the really colourful stuff that makes you you - **your VALUES.**

Values are things like behaviours, activities, preferences, beliefs - that are important to you and that you feel an instinctive pull towards.

Your values are **ANYTHING** that **you** value and consider are of worth.

They are an intrinsic part of **who you are** and represent your unique, individual self.

And to live your life aligned with your values is to know fulfilment.

So, could you name your top 5 or even 10 values?

It's not always easy to simply name your values off the top of your head, but it can be a useful thing to do.

There are many exercises online to get you started with this. You might decide to try out a few and compare the results.

Knowing your values is invaluable in making you aware of why you think and behave in the way you do.

However, just be on your guard for any value that you identify which doesn't *feel* quite right – there's a discord – you might even feel uneasy about holding this value.

This could be a value that 'you were given' as a child i.e. it was **someone else's value** that you adopted.

In recognising that this is **not** part of who you are, or want to be, you can let it go.

As your **self-awareness** grows, you may become aware of another voice – 'a bit wiser,' inner voice, which offers you good counsel. This is **your intuition** coming out to play.

Exciting stuff!

DO, however, bear in mind that **values** are quite different to **wants** and **needs**:

- a **need** is something you feel you *must* have – like food, information, a toilet, money…;

- a **want** is something that you *want* to acquire – like a holiday, a new car, a decent glass of wine…;

- but where there's a natural, uncomplicated pull at your very core – this is probably **value** driven.

A bit about ATTRACTION

The Law of Attraction, put simply, states that like attracts like.

It is based on the principle that each and every one of us is a source of energy – and that we emit vibrations (on a frequency) that draws *like* things towards us.

Whatever dominates your *thoughts* will *be* what is drawn towards you.

You are in essence a magnet!

So, if your thoughts are predominantly focussed on complaining and moaning about what is lacking in your life – this is what you will attract more of, i.e. *more lack*.

If you've never come across the **Law of Attraction** before, I'm sure this is sounding seriously 'woohoo,' so if this idea isn't speaking to you right now – that's fine.

But if it is, then maybe it's time to try this attraction exercise and see how it feels.

Think of an area in your life that you feel is lacking. Anything goes here: relationships, career opportunities, money, health…

Do you carry these thoughts around in your head all the time?

Is the situation so bad that you think about it first thing in the morning and last thing at night?

Does it even keep you awake?

The chances are that your thoughts are all about *'the lack'* and the impact of this lack on your life.

Ok let's turn the thinking around.

You need to start thinking about *abundance.*

The situation hasn't changed – YET.

But the thinking needs to.

Being stressed about a lack of anything is no joke and no fun, but you need to have some fun with this because you need to lighten your thinking and send out *'what you want to attract into your life'* on a *brand-new frequency*.

Just like in the good old days when you used to have to twiddle the knobs on the radio to find the station you were looking for.

What often stops people from fully embracing this is that they can't see HOW the abundance is going to come.

It is so important that you totally detach from any thoughts of HOW.

You simply need to let the attraction happen.

There may be ways in which abundance could come into your life that you are not even aware of: the opportunities, the people, the coincidences.

First - state clearly what you *want*: you need to be clear in your own mind what it is that you **want** to attract - remember don't focus on the how – just go for it.

Second - imagine how you will *feel* when you've got this: think about the things you will do - see yourself doing these things.

You need to **feel** the joy. Allow yourself to roll around in these joyful **feelings** – like pigs in muck!

You are now actively moving your energy to a higher (better) frequency.

Third - *believe* **it's on its way**: begin living your life **believing** that abundance is yours.

Expect things to go your way.

Expect abundance to come your way.

You are putting out the frequency that you are open for business.

You will start to see above the fog of lack to the place above.

You are up for success (whatever that means for you), fulfilment, and freedom from lack.

You just showed up **booted and suited**, to welcome abundance into your life.

R = Reality V Fake News

'The happiness of your life depends upon the quality of your thoughts...' **Marcus Aurelius**

Why challenge fake news?

Because if you don't - you could be wasting vast amounts of your precious time wrestling with thoughts that are keeping you trapped in **a circle of self-doubt**.

'Worrying does not take away tomorrow's troubles. It takes away today's peace.'

Randy Armstrong

There are many statistics bandied around – but a conservative suggestion is that something like 6,000 to 60,000 thoughts go through your mind in the course of a day.

Quite a thought!

HOWEVER, perhaps more mind-blowing than that is the suggestion that around 80% of your thoughts are **negative** and 95% are **repetitive** i.e. you are having the **same negative thoughts every single day!**

And thoughts packed with negativity fuel insecurity, fear, anxiety, and worry.

BUT the good news is that there is much that you can do to alter this, by simply improving the quality of your thoughts by separating out the fact from the fiction.

In other words, you need to **stop listening to the 'fake news'** which is robbing you of your creativity, self-belief, self-confidence, self-esteem, and self-worth.

So, why does your brain create these self-sabotaging thoughts?

Well, put simply, your brain doesn't 'think' it is giving you thoughts that are not in your best interest. It is creating thoughts in response to the stimulus it is receiving about **what it 'thinks' you want.**

There is no doubt that your brain is on your side. It's designed to keep you safe.

So, in times past, when you may have met a Sabretooth tiger on your way to the shops, the fight or flight response triggered in your brain (an automatic physiological reaction to a perceived threat) would have been perfectly appropriate and desirable.

The physical changes in your body would have had you totally wired for action – probably in this case to run.

HOWEVER, although nowadays the fight or flight response is still regularly triggered, it is usually due to quite different (psychologically stressful) situations that are not in themselves immediately life threatening.

In other words, there are times when a giant boulder is being called into action to simply crack a nut.

An example might help:

You've applied for a new job. You've got an interview. It's just the sort of job you've been longing for… AND THEN – you hear on the grapevine that this company has a notoriously tough interview process. There could be multiple rounds to this process. You might have to do a presentation. You're told that 'so and so' is also thinking about going for the job. She's supposed to be really good. Lots of people seem to like her…

Whoa there!

Time to slam the brakes on that runaway train – stuffed to the rafters with stories, opinions, and overthinking.

So, the message that your brain is receiving has gone *from* - excitement and joy at the prospect of landing this job – *to* *'this could be tough, I don't like doing presentations, I might* embarrass myself, 'so and so' is probably going to get the job anyway, lots of people seem to like her, maybe it would be for the best if I just withdraw…'

Your brain *now* thinks **ALERT** you're in danger, you don't really want this job, **I'm going to protect you** and fill your head with the sort of negative thoughts that you **need/want** to stop you going for it!

So, the job of your dreams just slipped through your fingers because you **'thought'** yourself right out of it.

'It begins in your mind, always. One moment you are feeling calm, self-possessed, happy. Then fear, disguised in the garb of mild-mannered doubt, slips into your mind like a spy.' Yann Martel

How to get started

Learn to challenge the thoughts that do not serve you.

These are YOUR thoughts.

They are in YOUR head.

So, it's down to **you** to **start coaching yourself** and get to grips with them.

<u>Learn to quiet the mind</u>

In the first instance it can be useful just to turn the volume down on all this crazy chattering inside your head.

You can stop feeding these thoughts by taking your attention away from them.

'A quiet mind can focus more objectively.'
Julie Starr

At the mention of **meditation** some people still raise an eyebrow and see it as a bit 'woohoo,' but like its close friend **mindfulness**, it is a powerful tool for bringing calm and relaxation to the mind and the body.

There's a ton of stuff on the internet and a mountain of books on both these subjects so check this out.

And remember, it's not smart to go poo-pooing either until you understand what they are, and what they offer. Remember **learning?** Your new best friend (first mentioned p 26).

Distract yourself

Distractions come in all shapes and sizes so you can get creative here in finding out what really does the business for you.

- **Music** – know your go to sounds.

- **Stories** – escape to another world through books or movies.

- **Physical stuff** – whatever rocks your boat – from yoga to marathon running.

- **Tap into nature** – this reminds you that you are part of something much much bigger.

- **Visualisation** – have that image at your fingertips – the one that instantly sparks joy when you see it.

You can have this on your phone, in your head, hanging on your wall – it doesn't matter what the format is just so long as you can summon it immediately when you need it.

When you focus on such a powerful (to you) image you are able to shift your mood and your thoughts. If it is a **place**, then imagine yourself in that place, on that beach, wherever it may be: Portobello, Whitby or the Maldives!

If it's an image of **someone**, then imagine you're with that person.

What you are looking for with distractions is every opportunity and means you can to starve these negative thoughts of your precious energy.

You're taking back control over your thoughts because you know that you should be the one in control. It makes no sense for you to be in the backseat allowing negatively-charged thinking, that's stuck on repeat, to be steering your life.

You know this intuitively.

REMEMBER: just because you're thinking something - doesn't make it true. Thoughts are just thoughts.

And if they're not serving you, you need to take **ACTION**.

You need to **challenge** them and **change** them.

The Reality v Fake News Sieve

Time to roll out those **fiction-busting questions** again (first mentioned p 29)

- Why do I think this?

- Where did this thinking come from?

- What are the facts?

- Where is the proof?

- Am I making assumptions?

These questions, and others just like them, make up your **Reality v Fake News Sieve** through which you can pour your chattering thoughts.

I think you will be surprised by how many of your troublesome thoughts are not based on fact.

Time to start trusting YOU to decide what is fact and what is fiction.

With the range and number of thoughts that are passing through your head in the course of a day you are not going to be able to challenge them all.

The good news is you don't have to. By taking yourself to the hard shoulder and observing your thoughts (not engaging with them) like watching cars flash by on a motorway – you can simply let them be.

Then pick your moment, decide on one particular train of

thought, and drop it into your sieve.

As you begin to recognise more clearly what is valid, and what is not, **you begin the process of taking back control.**

Your destructive thoughts will begin to lessen in number and

frequency because you are no longer supporting them through insecurity and fear.

As your **self-trust** and **self-belief** grows your default will change to being more confident in your ability to assess situations, people, thoughts, and opportunities in a more spontaneous and meaningful way.

I = Integrity First

'Telling the truth is a skill that may take several years to master. That's because telling the truth is something that doesn't always come naturally.' **Thomas Leonard**

If someone asked if you live your life with integrity, the chances are you will say 'yes,' before you've even thought about the question?

But I would stick my neck out here and say that for many of us the real answer would veer towards 'no,' or, at least, 'not always.'

Why integrity?

Because it makes life easier, sweeter, and more fulfilling. And it removes fear.

In accepting that we *don't* live with integrity as our constant bedfellow, we immediately raise our **awareness** and **empower** ourselves to allow a higher level of **honesty** into our lives - as and when we are ready.

How to get started

'Your ego is a false identity that your mind constructed and then you took up residence.' **Brandon Bays**

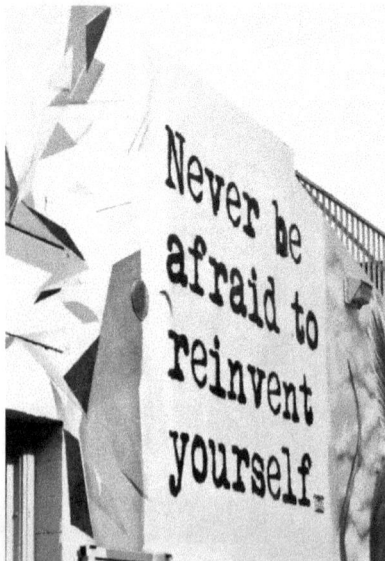

Start by being **honest with yourself about yourself.**

Do you try to appear like someone you're not?

Whilst pretence might make you look amazing to some – those who are more aware will spot the anomalies pretty quickly.

It's also exhausting and has a tendency to make you more serious, on your guard, and easily offended, because the fear of being exposed is ever present.

Do you recognise any of this?

So, if you live in a house, you can't *easily* afford, drive a car that's beyond your means, and check your bank balance mid-month with one eye closed - in the hope it won't look so bad - **then just STOP**.

Perhaps you feel it is impossible to step away from the façade that you've built.

But ask yourself how long can you keep this up before your **stress bucket overflows?**

Even if your level of pretence is on a much smaller scale than this – just telling a few porkies here and there about this and that – constantly lying is exhausting and a hard habit to break.

> 'Change your thinking and you will change your life.'
>
> **Brian Tracy**

BUT you still have a choice.

YOU always have a choice.

And yet, sometimes it is almost impossible to consider anything different to this manufactured version of your life, because you are so invested (and identified with) the façade you have created.

But you can liberate yourself. And you can coach yourself to do it in **your** own time, and on **your** own terms. So, consider stepping off the pretence treadmill.

REMEMBER the power of acceptance - total freedom to start again (first mentioned p 31).

Be your own genie, and give yourself the gift of contemplating an alternative way to live that aligns with **who you really are.**

'Integrity is doing the right thing, even when no one is watching.'

c s lewis

There's no need for any butt-clenching, embarrassing confession from the rooftops (unless you love a bit of amateur dramatics) as this is exactly what you've been peddling on that treadmill trying to avoid.

It is, therefore, perfectly possible to keep up the pretence whilst you get creative and start to explore *all* the possibilities of how to start this process of change.

The choice is yours.

It's up to you how you go about this. And how long it takes is purely dependent upon your circumstances, and the pace at which you decide to shed the shackles of your old life and make way for the new.

Integrity can be a hard-won prize, especially if you've strayed a long way from the real you - and it may well involve buckets of **courage** and a cup or two of **humility**.

But the lasting, life-enhancing benefits are spectacularly awesome:

- no longer scared of 'being found out' – you might even learn to **relax**

- **life feels easier** because you're not pretending anymore

- you **recognise falseness easily** – in others and yourself

- your inbuilt bullshit detector is now set to automatic

- you're **more fun - and more fun to be with** – the real you shows up more often

- your unique potential gets to flourish – you get to be **'the real deal'**

- you're able to **laugh at yourself and life** – you don't take yourself too seriously.

'Not a shred of evidence exists in favour of the argument that life is serious.' **Brendan Gill**

T =Tackling Tolerations

'Being flexible, adaptable, having gratitude – these are all virtues. But sometimes we operate at such a virtuous level that the virtues turn into vices.' Thomas Leonard

Why tackle tolerations?

Because tolerating things in your life, that erode your sense of wellbeing and self-worth need to stop.

'Free yourself from what does not serve you.'
Anon

For you to achieve that place of the best you, you need to start valuing who you are.

We are constantly asked, as human beings, to tolerate a number of things that we really don't want to.

This often starts when we are very young.

'Don't complain,' 'Don't rock the boat,' 'Stop putting yourself first,' 'You should start thinking about others,' 'Be grateful for what you have,' 'Be patient,' 'Stop whingeing,' and on it goes, the list is endless.

Now, in certain circumstances these comments may be appropriate. HOWEVER, there is a point beyond which being all-accommodating, and tolerating too many things, will start to sap your energy, diminish your self-esteem, and drain away your creativity and sense of joy.

By tolerating, you are essentially putting up with stuff that annoys and/or upsets you and as a consequence comprises your own happiness.

"The happiness of most people we know is not ruined by great catastrophes or fatal errors, but by the repetition of slowly destructive little things." **Ernest Dimnet**

How to get started

Just understanding that you may be tolerating situations that are bad for you is a start in itself, and can be a bit of a lightbulb moment.

You may have been feeling drained, wondered where all the joy went, but couldn't quite put your finger on the cause(s).

And the sneaky thing about tolerations is that they are often **compromises that *you've* talked yourself into accepting** - so you might need to dig around a bit to weed them out.

So, wake up time!

Start identifying the things that you do, or the things that you put up with, that drain your energy.

They can be big. They can be small.

Tap into that gut reaction.

If there's a discord in how you feel about something, then that something needs to be looked at.

Identified something?

Terrific!

So now what are you going to do about it?

- **First** - If there are a few – and there probably will be – list them. If there are many, then put them into categories i.e. work environment, home, pets, your habits and behaviour, partner's habits and behaviour, car etc.

- **Second** – Before you ditch a toleration make sure you understand why this toleration came about in the first place, so that you learn something from it *and* hopefully prevent it from reasserting itself in the future.

- **Third** – Ask yourself if there are any benefits to keeping a toleration? This might sound a bit of a contradiction after all the negative stuff I've just mentioned, but it is something to bear in mind. Do you tolerate a toleration because you benefit in some way – in other words, **is there a trade-off going on** here?

- **Fourth** – Don't use this exercise to start blaming **'every man and his dog'** for the fact that you have been tolerating these tolerations. Don't waste your time complaining.

Just start making plans to change things.

This is a learning process.

This is progress.

> 'Pushing through fear is less frightening than living with the underlying fear that comes from a feeling of helplessness'
>
> Susan Jeffers

The main thing is that you are now aware of tolerations, and their consequences.

You are in control, and you are making decisions about if/when, and how, you will deal with them.

It **can feel scary** to start tackling tolerations, so get a number of quick wins under your belt.

Start with some of the easier ones that perhaps involve you changing *your* behaviour e.g. a classic one would be that you are constantly late for appointments.

It makes you feel stressed.

You have to make excuses and tell little white lies.

It annoys you, but you keep doing it.

And it's never your fault, right?

Wrong!

I know how tough this one is. I've been there. But this is an example of something that irritates the hell out of you and is within your capacity to sort.

It's basically a bad habit caused by poor self-management.

So, just put your big grown-up pants on and deal with it!

Going up a good notch or two on the scary scale, however, could be tackling *someone else's bad behaviour* which you have tolerated for years.

And now you're going to make a **positive request** that they change the way they interact with you.

Start by understanding why you need this behaviour to change, and the effect it has on you.

Then **practise what you want to say to the other person.**

Gain strength from imagining how it will *feel* when this toleration has been eradicated.

You may find that a number of your tolerations are closely connected, and that when you tackle one it naturally leads to the next.

You may be thinking that it's not possible to fulfil all the roles in your life and effectively eliminate tolerations.

But the reason why *you can do this* is because you are learning how to respond to things **differently**.

You are building **self-confidence, self-awareness, and self-compassion**.

Value yourself more and others will do the same.

A bit about Self-Care

To be the best you can be, you need to feel good.

Seriously good!

Because when you feel good inside you radiate positivity, **self-esteem**, and **self-worth**.

Being 'selfish' has a bad press because virtually everyone uses this word to mean something negative.

And yet there are many times when **you should put yourself first**; especially if you've developed a chronic habit of consistently putting everyone else first.

The Chambers dictionary definition of selfish states:

'concerned excessively or exclusively with oneself: seeking or concentrating on one's own advantage, pleasure, or well-being <u>without</u> regard for others.'

I would suggest that the only word here that should cause you any real concern is 'without,' so now if you replace 'without' with 'with' and read that definition again it doesn't seem quite so *selfish,* does it?

The fact is that if you take care of yourself, you ARE doing it 'with regard for others,' because it's a **win/win** for everyone when you are at your best.

What I'm trying to illustrate here is that there are **NO benefits from undervaluing or devaluing your own worth.**

You do matter.

You are of extreme value.

You are a unique human being with extraordinary potential to do great things in this world for yourself and others.

So, the last thing that you should be doing is keeping yourself small.

Time to big it up - for everyone's sake!

And the reason for this is because when you nurture yourself to develop and grow in as many ways as your heart and mind can muster - you will find yourself in a **place of abundance**.

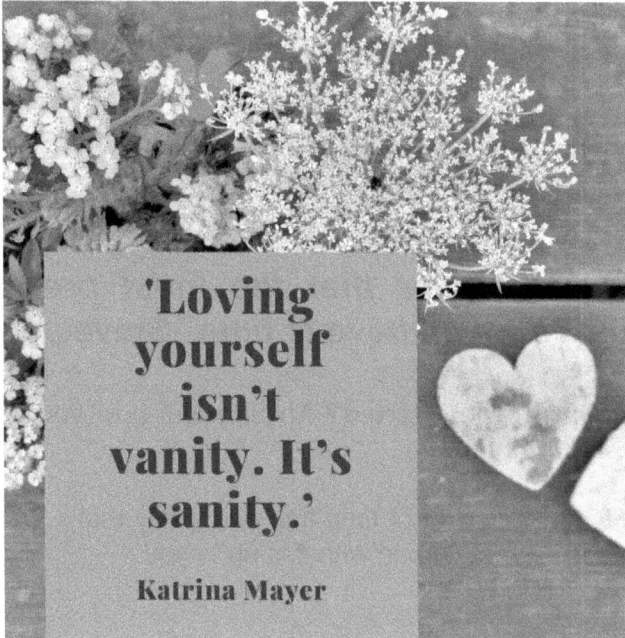

'Loving yourself isn't vanity. It's sanity.'

Katrina Mayer

You will need less help from others.

You will be more independent.

You will be in a position to be more generous to others.

When you care for yourself, everyone benefits.

So, start fine tuning everything in your life to ensure that **your mental health and wellbeing are your number one priority.**

Getting the right life/work balance that works for you, is both desirable and possible.

Checking in regularly with how you are **feeling** physically, and mentally, will let you know what needs attention and when.

REMEMBER you are, and always will be, your greatest asset - so it's time to give yourself some serious loving.

'It's really clear that the most precious resource we all have is time.' **Steve Jobs**

Struggling to get started? Think about how you spend your *precious* time?

- **Build** a pocket of time into every day that's **just for you** – what you do with it is up to you.

- **Stop** wasting your time doing things you don't want to do. **Start saying NO**. Practise makes perfect. This *will* get easier. **You *will* feel empowered.**

- **Make** treating yourself a habit. **Anything goes!** From a massage to a Mars bar.

Y =Yesterday is Gone

'The present moment is the liberator.'
Eckhart Tolle

Why focus on the present?

Because when you bind yourself to the **past** and/or the **future,** you're not allowing yourself to fully live in the **present.**

The past is gone.

Let it go.

It may hold valuable lessons. But don't use it as a means of self-flagellation.

If there are wounds, let them heal.

And equally, don't live with the **future** constantly on your mind.

Yes, planning and developing all manner of schemes in order to fulfil a future goal can be positive and desirable.

But is this where you focus *all* your energy and attention?

Are you *'absent without leave'* from the **here and now**?

For some, being overly focussed on the future can be a sign that they are not too happy with the present.

Whatever your vision of the future may be - **hold that vision lightly.**

Be flexible, open, and adaptable.

The future has a knack of taking care of itself.

<u>How to get started</u>

Put the three tenses in the correct order.

Each and every one of us is the product of our **past**.

We are, therefore, at any point in time, the sum total of what has gone before.

The past is exactly what it says on the tin – past and out of date.

If there are things in your past that you know (or suspect) are holding you back from living the life you want, start by making yourself **a timeline of your life.**

Don't overdo this, or dwell on anything unduly, just pick up the significant things that immediately come to you.

There may be things that you are already aware of - but **you might get bowled a googly**: something in your subconscious that you never suspected was there.

It might hit you like a blow to the stomach, if it comes accompanied with the emotions created at the time it took place.

You might have regrets about how you behaved or about how someone behaved towards you.

BUT don't be too hard on yourself or others.

Hindsight is a master at tormenting the life out of you.

'What if I'd done this…,' 'If only she'd done that…'

This is death by a thousand thoughts to your peace of mind!

REMEMBER who you were then, is not who you are now.

You did your best with the **level of awareness, knowledge, and experience** that you possessed at the time.

'Blame keeps you stuck in the past. Responsibility paves the path for a better future.'

Marilee Adams

And the same goes for anyone who caused you pain in the past.

So, do you want to say something to your past self, or to someone from your past?

This is about forgiving yourself and/or others for past behaviours.

So now you can write those letters to those people.

And I don't mean writing letters that rival 'War & Peace.'

Just get your thoughts and feelings down on paper.

Write it as it flows – like a stream of consciousness – no need to edit or embellish.

You may want to read it through once – but I would suggest – **only once**.

Then shred it or burn it.

Give these events permission to go back to where they belong – in the past.

Don't keep them to ruminate over at a later date.

This is a technique to put things to bed, not to develop new nightmares.

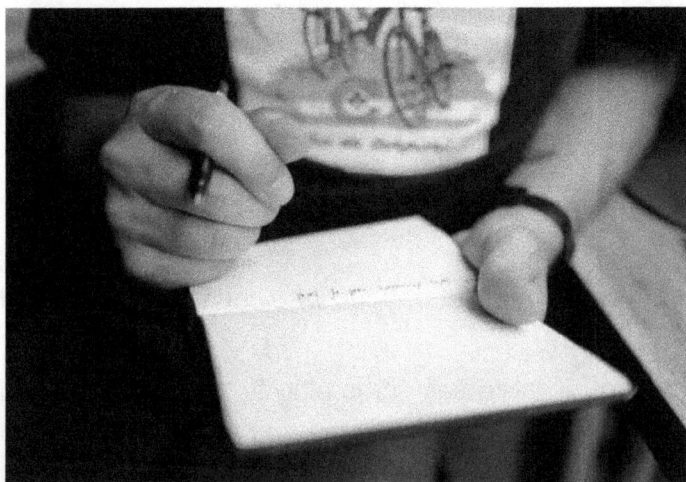

A bit about the PRESENT

This is where YOU are.

This is where YOU live.

This is the here and now.

So, how amazing would it be if you focussed your energy on just that – the here and now...

Allow yourself to explore this idea.

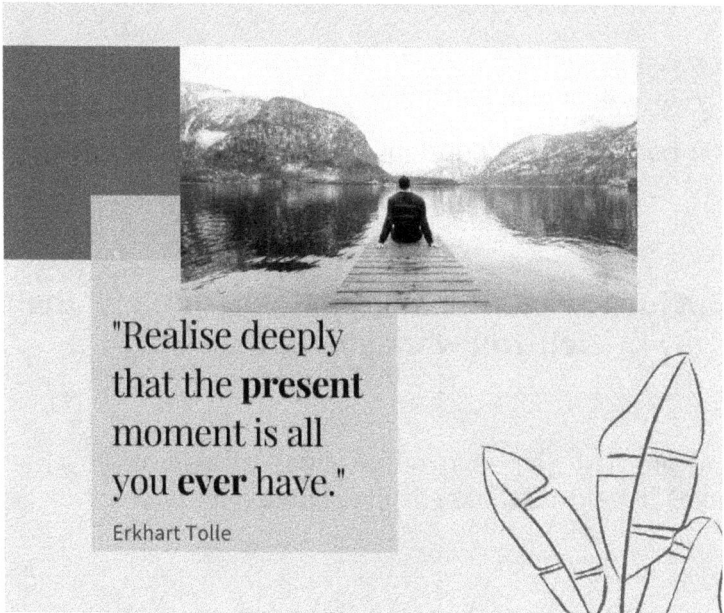

"Realise deeply that the **present** moment is all you **ever** have."

Erkhart Tolle

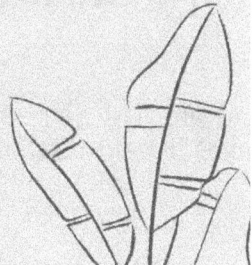

Don't be defensive with yourself – honesty is vital.

Look at your present situation again with new eyes.

Are you **grateful** for all that is good on your life?

When you actively think about what is good, and what you are grateful for, it shifts your perspective from lack to abundance.

This helps you to start from a place of **positivity** not negativity. AND if you're still not liking some (or all) of what you see, well, that's ok - because now, with your heightened (and ever-growing) level of consciousness, **you can start making changes.**

If you're not sure where to start, then you could try summoning another **perspective** to help out.

Maybe time to put those new 'objective' specs back on (first mentioned p 30).

Ask yourself what would an observer (total stranger) make of your present situation?

You could ask a friend that you trust implicitly, what they think?

But just be careful here that you don't let them tell you what you should do!

You are just gathering other points of view (if you need them) to help **YOU** assess the situation for yourself.

Trust yourself to find the best way forward.

Trust yourself to take care of yourself.

There is no one better...

> '**Maybe the journey isn't about becoming anything. Maybe it's about unbecoming everything that really isn't you - so you can become who you were meant to be...'**
> **Paulo Coelho**

AND a final word or two

So now it's over to you!

I hope you feel inspired to continue your self-coaching journey, and motivated to explore some of the ideas that I've presented here in more depth.

If you travel through life with **courage, curiosity, compassion, creativity,** and **kindness** I believe that you will find the clarity you are seeking to live your best life.

Namaste Ruth

Further Information

Below I have listed some of the **literature** and the **people** that have informed and inspired my self-coaching journey to date. I hope some of this proves useful.

Books

Adams, M. (2015) *Change Your Questions, Change Your Life (3rd ed)*, Berrett-Koehler

Bingham, E. (2025) *Manifest Your True Essence: Clear Your Blocks, Find Your Joy, Live Your Truth*, Hay House, London

Burkeman, O. (2011) *HELP!*, Cannongate

Byrne, R. (2000) *The Secret*, Simon & Schuster Ltd

Chopra, D (2007) *Seven Spiritual Laws of Success*, Amber-Allen

Choquette, S. (2008) *The Answer is Simple: Love Yourself, Live Your Spirit,* Hay House Ltd

Choquette, S. (2020) *Finding Trust in Your Inner Guidance System*, (Audiobook) Hay House UK

Choquette, S. (2021) *Ask Your Guides: Connecting to Your Divine Support System*, Hay House UK

Clear, J. (2018) *Atomic Habits*, Random House Business

Collard, Dr P. (2014) *The Little Book of Mindfulness*, Hachette UK

Collard, Dr P. (2019) *The Little Book of Meditation*, Hachette UK

Dispenza, Dr Joe (2012) *Breaking the Habit of Being Yourself*, Hay House

Dispenza, Dr Joe (2017) *Becoming Supernatural: How Common People Are Doing the Uncommon*, Hay House UK Ltd

Downey, M. (2003) *Effective Coaching (2nd ed)*, Thomson

Dyer, W. (2007) *Change Your Thoughts Change Your Life*, Hay House UK Ltd

Dyer, W. (2016) *Living The Wisdom of the Tao,* Hay House UK

Dyer, W. (2016) *10 Secrets of Success and Inner Peace,* Hay House UK

Edelman, Dr S. (2006) *Change Your Thinking With CBT*, Vermilion

Fiore, N. (2007) *The Now Habit*, Tarcher Perigee

Grosz, S. (2013) *The Examined Life: How We Lose and Find Ourselves*, Vintage

Haig, M. (2015) *Reason to Stay Alive*, Cannongate

Hicks, E & J. (2004) *Ask and It is Given*, Hay House

Hicks, E. & J. (2008) *The Astonishing Power of Emotions: Let Your Feelings Be Your Guide*, Hay House

Hill, N. (1937) *Think And Grow Rich,* The Ralston Society

Jeffers, S. (2012) *Feel the Fear and Do it Anyway*, Penguin Random Books UK

Kondo, M. (2014) *The Life-Changing Magic of Tidying*, Vermilion

Leahy, Dr R. L. (2005) *The Worry Cure: Stop Worrying and Start Living*, Piaktus

Leonard, T. J. (1998) *The Portable Coach*, Scribner

Luciani, J. (2004) *The Power of Self-Coaching*, Wiley & Sons

Luciani, J. (2016) *Thin from Within*, Amacom

McLeod, J. (2007) *Counselling Skill*, Open University Press

Morter, Dr S. (2020) *The Energy Codes*, Atria Paperback

Nguyen, J. (2024) *Don't Believe Everything You Think,* Authors Equity, New York

Osho, (2015*) Living Dangerously: Ordinary Enlightenment for Extraordinary Times*, Watkins

Roosevelt, E. (1960) *You Learn by Living: Eleven Keys for a More Fulfilling Life*, Harper Perennial

Russell, J. M. (2019) *A Brief Guide to Self-Help Classics*, Robertson

Ruiz, D. M. (1997) *The Four Agreements: A Practical Guide to Personal Freedom*, Amber-Allen Publishing

Segal, I. (2010) *The Secret Language of Your Body*, Atria Paperback, New York

Shetty, J. (2020) *Think Like A Monk,* Thorsons

Starr, J. (2016) *The Coaching Manual (4th ed)*, Pearson

Tolle, E. (2001) *The Power of Now: A Guide to Spiritual Enlightenment*, Yellow Kite

Tolle, E. (2005) *A New Earth: Create Your Better LifeToday*, Penguin Books, London

Watts, G & Morgan, K. (2015) *The Coach's Casebook: Mastering the Twelve Traits that Trap Us*, Inspect & Adapt Ltd

<u>People</u>

Jeffrey Allen, Michael Beckwith, Estelle Bingham, Gregg Braden, Deepak Chopra, Sonia Choquette, Peter Crone, Marie Diamond, Joe Dispenza, Wayne Dyer, Donna Eden, Louise Hay, Esther (Abraham) & Jerry Hicks, Ken Honda, Mark Hyman, Lewis Howes, Vishen Lakhiani, Danielle La Porte, Bruce Lipton, Joe Luciani, Gabor Mate, Mary Morrissey, Sue Morter, Nick Ortner, Marisa Peer, Bob Proctor, Tony Robbins, Don Miguel Ruiz, Inna Segal, Christie Marie Sheldon, Jay Shetty, Eckhart Tolle, Neale Donald Walsch, Oprah Winfrey

The best advice I can offer is to travel always with an **open mind** and step towards the ideas, tools and techniques that speak to you.

AND do be aware that there is a plethora of FREE quality material (masterclasses, taster courses and meditations) from many of the names I have listed above, on YouTube and on their personal websites.

www.ingramcontent.com/pod-product-compliance
Lightning Source LLC
Chambersburg PA
CBHW060532030426
42337CB00021B/4219